Struggle and Suffrage
in Manchester

Struggle and Suffrage in Manchester

Women's Lives and the Fight for Equality

Glynis Cooper

PEN & SWORD
HISTORY

AN IMPRINT OF PEN & SWORD BOOKS LTD.
YORKSHIRE - PHILADELPHIA

First published in Great Britain in 2018 by
Pen & Sword HISTORY
An imprint of
Pen & Sword Books Ltd
Yorkshire – Philadelphia

ISBN 978 1 52671 2 066

A CIP catalogue record for this book is
available from the British Library.

Printed and bound in England by CPI Group (UK) Ltd, Croydon, CR0 4YY

Pen & Sword Books Limited incorporates the imprints of Atlas, Archaeology,
Aviation, Discovery, Family History, Fiction, History, Maritime, Military,
Military Classics, Politics, Select, Transport, True Crime, Air World, Frontline
Publishing, Leo Cooper, Remember When, Seaforth Publishing, The Praetorian
Press, Wharncliffe Local History, Wharncliffe Transport, Wharncliffe True
Crime and White Owl.

For a complete list of Pen & Sword titles please contact
PEN & SWORD BOOKS LIMITED
47 Church Street, Barnsley, South Yorkshire, S70 2AS, England
E-mail: enquiries@pen-and-sword.co.uk
Website: www.pen-and-sword.co.uk

Or

PEN AND SWORD BOOKS
1950 Lawrence Rd, Havertown, PA 19083, USA
E-mail: Uspen-and-sword@casematepublishers.com
Website: www.penandswordbooks.com

Contents

Introduction

The Victorian period, despite having a queen on the throne for sixty-four years, proved to be one of the most repressive periods in British history for women. As queen, of course, Victoria would be used to having her requests obeyed and her needs provided for, but she appeared to remain blissfully unaware that she was virtually the only woman in the country for whom this was true. During much of her reign many women quite literally had fewer rights than a dog. Animal cruelty legislation was first mooted during the 1820s, but violence and cruelty towards women was not legally recognized for another thirty years and it was not until the 1870s that legal existence and rights for married women were enshrined in law. Before that time women were simply regarded as their husband's property (although obviously not in Queen Victoria's case), whose sole purpose in life was to be loving, patient, self-sacrificing and always understanding of their husband's every whim and desire at all times, regardless of their own feelings or situation. Deemed 'the Angel in the House' by Victorian poet Coventry Patmore, he wrote in 1844 that women should not even think about life after their husbands had died but should make every attempt to die of a broken heart. In 1941 this so enraged the writer Virginia Woolf that she declared 'killing the Angel in the House was part of the occupation of a woman writer.'

Nevertheless, during the century from 1850 to 1950 an enormous number of changes were made to the lives of women which eventually instigated the feminist movements of the 1970s and 1980s, seeking to establish equality and opportunity in all aspects of women's lives. It should have been a good and exciting time to be a woman but, as usual, history proved to be cyclical and old prejudices die hard. The most positive summary is that of 'two steps forward, one step back.' Progress has been made but at a price, and even today some Victorian attitudes can still be discerned just below the surface. A major step forward in the struggle came in 1918 with the granting of the vote to women aged over 30 followed by universal suffrage ten years later in 1928. The main initiative in the struggle for female emancipation and equality originated, unsurprisingly, in the millscapes of north-west England where hundreds of thousands of women in the nineteenth century suffered the most appalling living and working conditions, endured countless hardships and heartbreaks, struggled with high infant and maternity mortality rates, and prayed for death to release them from their suffering. Their plight was largely ignored by the establishment and by many men but not by their female contemporaries, some of whom were in more fortunate circumstances, and slowly the movement for change began to grow, challenging long-held views, gathering impetus, and culminating into the most tremendous show of solidarity, strength, support, ability and determination which finally enabled Britain to win the Great War. Their reward was female emancipation but that was only the beginning of the story. This book is a tribute to the countless thousands of women from Manchester and its townships, most of whom are anonymous and whose lives are lost in history, to celebrate their stoicism, their efforts and their contributions to 'sisterhood', helping women to take their place as first-class citizens rather than being relegated to second-class human beings.

Quite how and when the British started to disrespect, dislike and dismiss their womenfolk as second-class citizens is lost in the mists of time. Anglo-Saxon women certainly had greater freedoms in many respects than their later counterparts and there are sweet romantic visions of early medieval troubadours singing love songs to woo the girls of their dreams. In later medieval times, however, women were often regarded simply as pawns to be used in empire-building through advantageous marriages and by the time of Henry VIII no one raised much protest when he had two of his six queens beheaded. The reduction to second-class citizen status for women, as advocated by the patriarchal Abrahamic religions of Christianity, Judaism and Islam, may well have been encouraged by the Norman invasion of 1066. France is a Catholic country and the Catholic Church gained in ascendancy over the indigenous Celtic Church after the Conquest. The Catholic Church is strongly patriarchal and attributes all original sin to Eve; i.e. woman. Although Henry VIII replaced Catholicism with the Church of England in 1534, many of the old religious views remained and, even today, the Church of England does not easily embrace women as equal citizens.

Britain is also one of the most class-conscious countries in the world. The Industrial Revolution, which really began to gather steam in the late eighteenth century, was a major catalyst for the whole question of 'class'. Before this date 'class' tended to be based on hereditary characteristics such as family, rank, estate ownership, hierarchy within religious orders, etc. One of the constant beliefs of the upper classes was that 'old families' must be preserved at all costs. All families are 'old' in the sense that they must have had ancestors back into pre-history or they would not exist today. People don't just appear from nowhere. What was really meant was that 'old families' could trace their lineage back several generations; a few as far back as the Conquest which was when titles and large estates were handed out as rewards to those who had fought well for the winning side. It was generally accepted that a lot of 'class' was due to bloodline, with the royal family and those at the top of the upper-class tree often being referred to as 'blue-blooded'. The reality is rather more prosaic. There are four main blood groups: A, B, AB and O, each with rhesus positive and rhesus negative divisions. No single blood group is unique to any one class of people and all human blood is red. Ironically, some living creatures such as spiders, crabs, squid, octopus and a number of invertebrates do actually have blue blood due to using haemocyanin rather than haemoglobin to circulate their oxygen supply. Although science had not yet fully explained these basic facts in the late eighteenth century, changes had begun to occur and, with the advent of the Industrial Revolution, wealth and income became the major criteria for 'class' rather than 'breeding', i.e. a long-recorded 'noble' lineage, although those who bought in were sometimes sneeringly referred to as the 'nouveau riche'. There are precedents far back in pre-history for a social hierarchy based on personal wealth. Archaeology has shown that farming settlements in the New Stone Age were collections of evenly-sized evenly-placed dwellings, and bartering, not money, was the form of exchange for goods. Some folk were better hunters or better farmers; others could make better baskets or weapons or pottery. Meat and wheat could be exchanged for spears, baskets and bowls. The discovery of precious metals turned the social order upside-down as folk who owned anything made from these coveted metals were looked up to, admired and somehow considered to be better persons.

Possession became important. Settlements in the Bronze Age and the Iron Age that followed show one or two large dwellings surrounded by a few much tinier ones that could only have been hovels. Bronze Age chieftains used their metal wealth to obtain large tracts of land and built themselves ostentatious tombs from where they could look down on their former estates after death. Then, somewhere around 500/600BC, someone invented money. Goods or services could then be paid for through exchanges of small metal discs, and the concept of capitalism had begun.

Capitalism is largely led by market demand and relies, for its success, on making profits for those who invest cash or assets. Those with the largest amount of money or assets can afford to invest the most and will, therefore, make the most profit. In order to maximize profits it is necessary to minimize outgoings, and it did not take long to discover that workers' wages were the easiest target to minimize. Slave labour was used for centuries in many societies, but it was gradually outlawed throughout Britain and her Empire after the Slavery Abolition Act was passed in 1833. Those who worked for a wage did so because they needed to provide food, clothing and shelter for themselves and their families. They mostly had no assets and, in a possessive and materialistic society, were therefore looked down upon and regarded as being at the bottom of the social hierarchy. As such, they were deemed to have no power and little value. It was easy to pay them the lowest of low wages for working exceedingly long hours. However, the working classes did have one huge asset that was much in demand. As realization dawned on workers throughout the nineteenth century that their labour was essential to keep the wheels of industry turning and the capitalist system in place, their confidence grew in demanding better wages, better conditions and better rights. Men often earned nearly twice as much as women and reserved the right to their own wages. Until 1870 women's wages automatically belonged to their husbands. For a minimum twelve-hour day, five and a half days a week – equalling a sixty-six-hour week – men earned the modern equivalent of £1.28 per hour (boys received 48p per hour), while women only earned 71p per hour (girls received 35p per hour) for the same type of work. Moreover, at the end of a long working day men had the expectation of relaxing, having a meal put on the table for them and then going out to the pub for a drink and socializing. Women came home from a long day in the mills, factories or 'sweat-shops' and were expected to cook, clean, wash and care for their children, and they had no 'mod cons' or labour-saving devices. If they refused, many could expect a good beating. As late as 1906 a government report indicated that mill and factory-owners preferred the use of female labour, not only because their wages were much lower than those of men but because women 'could be more easily induced to undergo severe bodily fatigue than men.' It was a sad fact that control, abuse, economic deprivation and violence were the order of the day for many Victorian women from all classes.

This then was the background against which the struggle was fought for universal franchise, career opportunities, decent wages, equal civic and human rights for all women. In many respects the women of Manchester led the way because there were so many strong and resilient characters among them and they had suffered far more ill-treatment, deprivation, degradation and sheer brutality than much of the rest of the country, mainly due to the sheer size and success of Cottonopolis. In 1750 Manchester had a population of just 20,000 people. Around 100 years later this had multiplied more than twelve times to 250,000. By 1950 it had fallen to around 183,000, mainly due to the collapse of the cotton industry. Despite reducing numbers, Manchester women continued to remain strong and resilient characters. They had learned from their mothers and grandmothers the determination needed for sheer survival. They had helped to build an affluent and prestigious country. They had learned the value of strong and lasting relationships within the 'sisterhood'. This culminated in their biggest achievement of all: changing the course of history so that it became 'her-story' as well as 'his-story'.

CHAPTER ONE

Education and Training

There had been protests since the 1770s (the beginnings of the Industrial Revolution) about the declining quality of education and these continued for 100 years until the passing of the 1870 Education Act. Girls 'of gentle birth' were educated at home, which meant basic competency in the 'three Rs' of reading, (w)riting and (a)rithmetic, followed by what were seen as essential feminine accomplishments of music, dancing, singing, sewing, embroidery, flower-arranging and painting in water colours. For the boys from wealthier homes there were grammar schools and public schools where they received a decent general education and a grounding in the classics.

For poorer children there were church schools, Sunday schools, parish schools and, especially in Manchester with its rapid urban growth, 'ragged schools' (charity schools), which provided basic education, religious teaching, food and clothing to children 'too ragged to go to other schools.' Many children were either illiterate or semi-literate, although literacy was very important in so many respects, not least of which was the ability to read warning notices in mills and manufactories. There were two ragged schools on Charter Street and Sharp Street that catered for children from Angel Meadow, one of the most deprived and squalid districts in the millscapes of Manchester. However, many fathers from all strata of society saw little point in educating their daughters much since they were simply destined for marriage and domestic chores. In lower-income households there was the added incentive of needing to get children into work as soon as possible to lessen the burden on the main wage earner/s for the number of mouths it was their responsibility to feed. There was also the question of time for learning. Until the 1840s children from the age of 5 could work up to fourteen hours a day in the mills. A few mill-owners, more philanthropic than their colleagues, tried to genuinely care for and, at least partially, educate their child 'apprentices' as they were euphemistically called. Quarry Bank Mill, close to the present Manchester Airport, had an apprentice house where its working children lived. They slept in same-sex pairs on truckle beds and received one decent meal a day after work, being given slabs of stiff onion-flavoured porridge to eat during the day while they worked. In the evening, after they had eaten, both girls and boys were given an hour's educational instruction, followed by an hour during which the girls sewed clothes for themselves and the boys, while the boys worked in the kitchen garden that supplied vegetables for their meals. A local doctor, who happened to be the uncle of the novelist Elizabeth Gaskell, attended to their medical needs and his casebook survives. They saw little of their parents, perhaps twice a year, and the girls in particular missed their mothers very much. The mothers missed their children as well, but understood that in the economic conditions under which they were forced to live it was the best if not the only way.

Unlike their better-off sisters, many working-class women simply had no time for educational activities, but during the mid-nineteenth century a breakthrough of a kind was achieved. In 1844 the Twelve Hours Act was passed, followed by the Ten Hours Act in 1847, which limited the number of hours an individual could be forced to work in any one day. Any extra hours would count as 'voluntary overtime'. There was a great deal of furious reaction, mostly from men. For women it could only have been a relief since, when they went home from a full day working in the mills, the duties of cooking, cleaning and childcare fell to them as their husbands relaxed with a newspaper or went to the pub. Then, three years later in November 1850, Salford Museum and Art Gallery opened as 'The Royal Museum & Public Library'.

It was the first free public library in England, followed in 1852 by the library in Campfield, Manchester becoming the first library to operate a free lending service. Charles Dickens called public libraries 'the great free school'. Finally, some degree of self-education through books and reading was available to everyone, regardless of gender or class. Nine years later the American Civil War (1861–65) broke out over the use of slaves on the cotton plantations. Manchester men and women supported the struggle against slavery, although it was the beginning of the end for the British cotton industry.

The passing of the Education Act 1870 guaranteed a compulsory basic education for all children between the ages of 5 and 12. The Act met with some considerable resistance from those who had 'vested interests in keeping the population ignorant and in want' because if folk received an education they might then have the skills or articulation either to obtain other work or to lobby for improvements in wages and working conditions in the millscapes. Besides, it would also take them out of the labour market until they were aged 12. In any case, the scope for female education was still very limited and girls were often intellectually frustrated. Elsie Furlong, born in 1890, was the daughter of a pawnbroker in Cheetham Hill. Although the family could afford to have a servant living in, Elsie's father decided that he either could not or would not afford secondary education for her after the age of 12. Disappointed, Elsie gained herself an extra couple of years by becoming a pupil teacher until she was 14 but then she had to leave school and find work. She was a bright, attractive girl with interests in politics and amateur dramatics, and she keenly felt the injustice of being denied further education through an accident of birth. She supported the suffragette movement and was delighted when female emancipation was finally granted, but by then she was married with a young family and a part-time job in her husband's firm. Although she continued to take a lively and active part in politics and current affairs, the chance of further or higher education had passed her by. As work in the cotton mills declined, it became obvious that new skills would be needed for folk to find work elsewhere. There was a thriving engineering industry in Manchester, and it was the heyday of the railways. While initially this affected boys more than girls, there was a growing demand for 'education of Manchester's daughters similar to that provided for Manchester's sons', and in 1874 the Manchester High School for Girls was established in the city centre suburb of Chorlton-on-Medlock. Manchester Grammar School was, and still is today, strictly for boys only.

The University of Manchester Institute of Science and Technology (UMIST) had its origins in the Manchester Mechanics Institution, founded in 1824, as 'part of a national movement for the education of working men.' The Medical School originated as a private medical school but became part of Owens College in 1872. This institution was also essentially for men. Owens College was founded in 1851 and from the 1860s onwards also embraced research as well as teaching faculties. However, it was difficult for females to undertake educational research projects and, even if they did, they were often blocked purely on account of their sex as Beatrix Potter (the internationally-acclaimed children's author) discovered to her cost. Although she was born and brought up in London, her entire family (with the exception of her paternal grandmother who was Lancastrian) came from the Manchester area and Beatrix always regarded herself as a northerner. Her parents were affluent, but Beatrix was a talented artist and she wanted to do something useful with her life. Each summer her parents rented houses in the country or on the coast for long summer holidays and Beatrix became fascinated by a variety of mushrooms which still grew wild in the fields, woods and hedgerows. She drew and painted them all in very accurate detail. Curious as to how they reproduced, she studied fungal spores and wrote a treatise on the subject. No one had done this before, so it was a piece of original research. Excitedly she applied to read her paper to the Linnean Society which was dedicated to the study of natural history and evolution. Her request was refused simply because she was a woman but her uncle, Sir Henry Roscoe, a distinguished Manchester chemist, was appalled by the society's decision and arranged to have her paper read to them by a man. It received a lukewarm reception because, after all, what could a mere woman know about such scientific matters? Beatrix was advised to go back to writing her children's stories about cute little animals. She was dreadfully disappointed but she realized that there would be no future for her in the study of fungi. It is said that revenge is a dish best eaten cold and Beatrix finally achieved her ambition to do something that she regarded useful with her life. Using the money she earned from writing her children's books she bought a farm in the Lake District and, in 1913, she married William Heelis, the solicitor who had helped her with the conveyancing. From that moment on she gave up writing children's books and she insisted on being known as Mrs Heelis. No one was to call her Beatrix Potter any more. It was her ambition to become a respected breeder of Herdwick sheep, a notoriously difficult breed, and this was how she wanted to be remembered. In 1914 Queen Mary asked Beatrix if she would design and paint Christmas cards for the Royal family. Beatrix declined, much to her mother's utter horror. That part of her life was over and now she wanted to be taken seriously. She would not be fobbed off again to paint little cuties. She was going to be useful.

In 1899 Enriqueta Rylands, the wife of wealthy Manchester mill-owner John Rylands, founded and endowed the John Rylands University Library on Deansgate in memory of her late husband and, in 1900, Owens College finally became the Victoria University of Manchester. A college education rapidly became desirable for those entering the professions, but there was some considerable delay in admitting women to higher education. Even by the end of the nineteenth century, school curriculums still advocated that only 'domestic' subjects should be taught to girls along with basic literacy and numeracy, while boys were given a wealth of choice. In 1883 Owens College grudgingly admitted women 'on a five-year trial basis' but it was another fourteen years before women were admitted to all degree examinations 'except those in engineering and medicine'. Esther Roper was one of the first women to read for a degree at Owens College. She was admitted in 1886 as part of the scheme to assess 'whether females could study without harm to their mental or physical health' and in 1891 she graduated with a first-class honours degree in Latin, English Literature and Political Economy. While at college she helped to edit *Iris*, a twice-yearly publication for female students highlighting issues in women's education. After leaving college she worked as secretary of the Manchester National Society for Women's Suffrage (NSWS) where she tried to involve working-class women as much as middle-class females in the cause. There was still prejudice against women in certain educational matters and it continued into the following century. As late as the 1960s, in many schools boys did not take domestic science classes and girls did not take woodworking classes. Even in the twenty-first century, there is still a distinct lack of female engineers and engineering remains one of the most unpopular subjects among schoolgirls.

By 1900, however, females represented around 16 per cent of the university population and by 1910 it was one in five. Before the Great War many girls going to university anywhere had to commit to being a teacher to get a grant because teaching was still one of the very few careers open to them. Women had made a great deal of progress to gain access to higher education, but many colleges and universities still regarded themselves as bastions of masculinity. Even in Manchester, women at college were teased and bullied, barred from certain clubs and societies, and forced to live and work in segregated quarters that were often substandard. Nevertheless, most regarded it as a small price to pay for their achievements. Unfortunately, it is a price that has continued to be paid. The Oxbridge universities still have exclusively male-only organizations, usually based on drinking clubs, (the Bullingdon Club and the Piers Gaveston drinking society in Oxford; the Wyverns and the notorious Pitt Club in Cambridge). Their members see females purely as sex objects for whom depravity and lust should be the only reasons for toleration, while their antics support Einstein's assertion that there are no limits to human stupidity.

Before the Great War (1914-18) boys regularly attended evening classes in technical subjects but, although girls were free to do the same, many attended classes in domestic subjects such as cookery, dress-making, hygiene, childcare, etc. because marriage, children and the home remained idealized objects of female attainment. It would also fit them for a life 'in service', working in country houses as servants of the rich and privileged for low wages and little time off. It was the Great War that finally broke the mould on education and training for women, especially in Manchester. As the men marched off to war in their thousands, women hastened to fill the void they had left in the mills, manufactories, transport and administration systems. Although there was only time for minimal training, they learned the basic principles of jobs quickly and proved themselves adaptable and efficient, acquiring new skills and new confidence. Girls left the mills and domestic service in droves to work in munitions factories for decent wages and to help the war effort, despite the inherent dangers and the all-too-brief training they received. Women were trained to take over roles in shops and offices, and some even learned to drive. In 1917 the Land Army was set up with more than a quarter of a million women willing to work on farms to ensure maximum food production for the country. Land Army workers spent one month in assisted training before being sent out to work in all weathers and undertaking all manner of tasks. They undertook anything, from ploughing and harvesting to milking cows and mucking out pigs. Their main problem was male criticism but even hard-to-please farmers professed themselves impressed. Nursing became a respectable vocation, like many other occupations. Domestic servitude was no longer seen as a career.

This revolution in female education and training, adaptability and efficiency did not stop ugly incidents, however. In Manchester, female tram conductors were spat upon by men who thought they should be at home in their kitchens, and some Manchester men refused to be served by females in shops and offices. The unkindest cut of all was when the war ended and women were told to leave their jobs so that men returning home from the armed forces could have them. If they refused, women could be assaulted, beaten and, on occasion, even raped.

The end of the Great War heralded a new era for female education in Manchester. Women were no longer barred or discouraged from attending schools, universities and colleges, or studying for qualifications and degrees. Ellen Wilkinson and Dame Kathleen Ollerenshaw are two outstanding examples from the early twentieth century of what could be achieved through allowing women access to higher education. Ellen Wilkinson was born in 1891 in the inner-city slum suburb of Chorlton-on-Medlock. Her father combined strong views on social justice and self-help, ensuring that his children received a good education and learned to read widely. In 1906 Ellen began training as a teacher at the Manchester Day Training School, spending half her time in college and half teaching at Oswald Road elementary school. However, she refused to impose learning by rote and subsequently decided that teaching was not the career for her. Impressed by the principles of socialism, she joined the ILP (Independent Labour Party) and, after meeting Hannah Mitchell, began supporting the women's suffrage movement. In 1910 Ellen won the Jones Open History Scholarship and was awarded a place at Manchester University. Once there she joined the Fabian Society and the Manchester Society for Women's Suffrage. After leaving university she worked as a trade union organizer and then went into politics, still actively campaigning for equal opportunities and equal pay for equal jobs for women. She was MP for Middlesbrough from 1924 to 1931 and for Jarrow from 1935 to 1947, leading the Jarrow Hunger March in 1936. In August 1945 she became Minister of Education in Clement Attlee's government; only the second woman to hold a Cabinet position. Her main achievement was the implementation of the 1944 Education Act providing free education for all children and raising the school leaving age to 15. She also initiated the 11+ examination, although this alienated many socialist colleagues who saw the system whereby an exam at age 11 would determine whether a child would go to grammar school, 'modern' school or technical school as 'perpetuating elitism' and who wanted a comprehensive system of education that would see children of all abilities taught under one roof, if not in one class.

Dame Kathleen Ollerenshaw was born Kathleen Timpson in Withington, an outer south Manchester suburb, in 1912. She became deaf at the age of 8 but she attended Lady Barn House School where she became passionately interested in maths. She went to Somerville College, Oxford in 1931 to read mathematics, gaining her degree three years later, and then, in 1945, her doctorate. After the Second World War she worked at Manchester University part-time as a lecturer in the maths department while bringing up her children (both of whom predeceased her). She was also active in educational matters, initiating the creation of the Royal Northern College of Music and advising Margaret Thatcher's government on education, as well as serving as the president of St Leonard's School in St Andrews, Fife, from 1981 to 2003. She was also the President of the Institute of Mathematics and its applications, publishing at least twenty-six papers on the subject. She received her damehood in 1970 for services to education. Keenly interested in politics, she was a Conservative councillor for Rusholme from 1956 to 1981, becoming Lord Mayor of Manchester from 1975 to 1976 and High Sheriff of Greater Manchester from 1978 to 1979, and she was also made a Freeman of the City.

Manchester, like almost every other town and city in Britain, understood that since the Great War a lost generation of skilled and experienced working men needed to be replaced, and that women had proved themselves capable of ameliorating the skills shortage. Just twenty years later another global conflict saw women, out of necessity, training for the armed forces, for secret government work and for positions of responsibility on an unprecedented scale. As the twentieth century continued, it became acceptable for women to have a university education and to enter professions such as the law, medicine, dentistry, veterinary practice, the higher levels of teaching, accountancy, etc. The main problems, after the establishment of equal educational and training opportunities for women, were the question of equal pay for both sexes for equal jobs, and the creation of a 'glass ceiling', as it came to be known, in many spheres of work, imposing a certain level beyond which women could not be promoted. Although in the first decades of the twenty-first century this situation still exists to some extent, it has not deterred women from continuing the struggles of their mothers, grandmothers and great-grandmothers for a wiser, less prejudiced environment in which future generations of girls can work, study and achieve educational ideals.

CHAPTER TWO

Working and Childcare: Domestic Service, Home-Working, Factories, Offices, Shops, Changes in the First and Second World Wars

Until the coming of the Industrial Revolution, career options for women were extremely limited. Their main goal was a good marriage and working-class girls were expected to have the 'womanly virtues' of being able to cook, clean and sew. If they needed to go out to work, going into domestic service was practically the only option. A few might work from home as local washerwomen or seamstresses, but most 'went into service' which meant obtaining a place in one of the big country houses. Many would start as a scullery maid and work their way up. They were given food, accommodation and a uniform, but wages were exceptionally low and time off even lower; one Sunday off per month was considered generous. The prettier girls might also become objects of attention from the sons of the house. These lads could never offer them marriage because up until the twentieth century and even beyond, marrying 'out of class' was simply not done. If a girl who was a maid turned down overtures from 'one of those upstairs', she could be sacked for insubordination. If she agreed to a relationship and became pregnant, she was sacked from her job with no reference. Either way, she was the loser. For girls from the emerging middle class, the daughters of professional men, the clergy, or wealthier merchants, virtually the only career open to them, if they were unfortunate enough to need to earn their own living, was that of being a governess to other people's young children. They were also expected to have additional 'feminine accomplishments' such as being able to play the piano, sing, draw, paint and to have achieved a decent standard in embroidery. For upper-class girls, a good marriage really was the only option since any kind of work would denigrate their social standing and their family's position in the hierarchy of the nobility.

The Industrial Revolution, spearheaded by the Manchester cotton mills, caused a massive social upheaval for both sexes but especially for women. Manchester had ideal climatic conditions for the cotton manufacturing industry which expanded rapidly during the century following its inception during the early 1770s. Rural life on farms or in villages was depressed at this time and, encouraged by stories of good wages and better living conditions in the city, country folk migrated to Manchester in their thousands, hoping for the chance of a better life. Cotton mill-owners were delighted. The reality, of course, was rather different. There was great competition for jobs so it was an employers' market, useful for holding down wages. Cotton mill life was very different and was regimented by the clock. Queues of people wanting work formed outside the factory gates by 6.00 am every day. Those who were not punctual could find the gates were closed by 6.01 am. It came as a great shock to country folk mentality, for the cows had never minded whether they were milked at 6.00 am, 6.15 am or 6.30 am as long as they got milked, and it is said that this absolute adherence to the very minute was responsible for the British obsession with the clock and punctuality. The mills have long gone but the mindset has not. For once, women often had the advantage in that their fingers are smaller and nimbler than those of men, so were often better suited to the spinning and weaving procedures, and they could be paid less than men. Better still, they could bring their children with them; although they would work for even less wages, every penny was welcome. It cost money to shut down cotton manufacturing machinery for cleaning and children were small enough to be able to crawl underneath the machinery while it was still moving to clean and de-fluff the moving parts. Health and safety was totally ignored and, of course, there were numerous accidents, but many employers considered workers' children totally expendable. There were always more to fill the vacancies. The hours were long, however, and the wages less than had generally been expected. A survey by the *Journal of the Statistical Society* in 1859 records the average wages for cotton operatives in Manchester and Salford:

- average earnings for a man working a 66-hour week (5 x 12-hour days plus Saturday mornings) was 18s 6d (approx. £84.60 in modern values).
- average earnings for a woman working a 66-hour week (5 x 12-hour days plus Saturday mornings) was 10s 2d (approx. £46.90 in modern values).
- average earnings for a boy working a 66-hour week (5 x 12-hour days plus Saturday mornings) was 7s (approx. £32.20 in modern values).
- average earnings for a girl working a 66-hour week (5 x 12-hour days plus Saturday mornings) was 5s (approx. £23.00 in modern values).

Although the 10 Hours Bill had been passed just over a decade earlier there was nothing to stop employees agreeing voluntarily to work longer hours and, if asked, what choice did they have? Many had left jobs and tied cottages in the countryside and there was no going back. In the city there were always others ready to take over their jobs, and if they left because of refusing to work longer hours they would not get a decent reference. It was simply Hobson's choice for most folk.

Women, although they worked as hard, earned far less than men but at this time married women could not own anything they earned and their wages went straight to their husbands. The same was true for their children. Some husbands were decent men who cared for their families and gave their wives adequate housekeeping allowances. However, some women never knew whether they would get a hand-out or a beating. Some mill-owners paid some of their workers' wages 'in kind' with tokens that could be exchanged for food and sundries at certain shops; these were maintained and stocked by the mill-owners so the prices of goods might not be the most economical. There was also a growing engineering industry developing in Manchester during the latter half of the nineteenth century, and there was great demand from trade for transportation facilities to be provided as well as a boom in the building of railways. However, the engineering and transport industries remained closed to women until the Great War.

Drink and the use of opium became big social problems as the awfulness of living and working in Manchester took its toll and folk tried to find relief, albeit temporary, from their grim and often hopeless circumstances. Friedrich Engels described what it was like living in the city in his book *The Condition of the Working Class in England*. Central Manchester was 'a place of filth, ruin and uninhabitableness…it was…hell upon earth…' A pall of smoke and smog hung constantly over the city so that the sun was only seen as a dim red disc giving little light. Health and safety regulations did not exist. The noise in the mills was such that sign language had to be used between operatives. The noise of a working mill, like Quarry Bank Mill near Manchester Airport, is so loud that today no one is allowed more than ten minutes' exposure to it. Home for many workers was cramped, crowded, often damp, sanitation facilities were, at best, extremely limited and any comforts were almost non-existent. Even poor farm labourers had been accustomed to something better on the land. One unexpected casualty of the mass migration to the towns was the demise of cottage industries such as weaving and spinning by hand for the women and woodworking and pottery-making by the men, which had maintained old skills and earned a few extra pence.

The plight of working children in Manchester and other British towns was condemned throughout Europe. They worked longer hours in worse conditions than the slave children of America. Mothers cried in despair. This was not what they had expected. Children too young to work were put with nurses who gave them laudanum to keep them quiet. Their parents often worked at least twelve hours a day and five and a half days a week for little benefit to themselves or their families. The novelist Elizabeth Gaskell did for the mill-workers of Manchester what Charles Dickens had done for the poor of London. In her novels she highlighted the savage conditions under which workers were born, lived and died, often well before their time. A few of the more philanthropic businessmen and mill-owners suggested that working folk were so tired they were not giving of their best and that a shorter working day might be beneficial to all. For the most part this fell on deaf ears, although as early as 1810 a Welshman named Robert Owen, who set up his business in Manchester, conceived the notion of an eight-hour day: 'eight hours' labour, eight hours' recreation, eight hours' rest.' He practised this in his own factories but, unsurprisingly, the idea was not generally popular. However, things clearly could not continue as they were. In 1844 a Bill was passed limiting the working day to twelve hours which was followed by another Bill in 1847 further limiting working hours to ten per day. This was met with howls of fury and protest from mill-owners and most of their male workers, but some sighs of relief from female and child workers. After all, they were the ones who came home and had to start work all over again. Finally, in 1870, the Education Act was passed making education compulsory for all children until the age of 12 and it marked the end of child slave labour.

The breakthrough in childcare for the under-5s came with the Great War. Mindful of the urgent task of replacing the 'lost generation' with a new, intelligent and healthy generation, lateral thinking was applied to the problem and the idea of nursery education for children aged 2 to 5 was born. The 1918 Education Act, more commonly known as the Fisher Act after its instigator Herbert Fisher, was passed in August 1918. It charged local education authorities with attending to the 'health and physical condition of the children' as well as to their educational needs, requiring them to provide holiday camps, medical inspections, resources for children with special needs and free nursery schools for children aged 2 to 5. Manchester was one of the first cities in the country, along with London, Edinburgh and Birmingham, to offer free nursery education for its infants. The city built on this foundation and there were a number of local innovations in the provision of nursery care for the under-5s during the following decades. It was officially recognized that the first few years of a child's life were the most important years in terms of development.

The Great War was also a huge breakthrough for the female labour market. So many men were called up to fight at the fronts that females filled their places in shops, offices, factories, munitions manufacture, transport services, public services, catering, forestry, agriculture; the list was endless. Female workers proved themselves adaptable, capable, competent and fast learners. One of the toughest tasks had been that facing the Women's Land Army who had to prove to conservative farmers, most of whom were campaigning for their sons to be brought home from the front to assist in farm work, that they could do any task on the farm just as effectively and efficiently as men. They succeeded, earning the respect of many men, including those in the government and industry, for their competence and hard work in so many different spheres of employment.

Gone were the old stereotypes of domestic servants and governesses. Female domestic servants deserted their posts in droves. This happened all over the country as well as in Manchester and it was an unexpected consequence of the Great War that the Victorian and Edwardian country house way of life, depicted so well by *Downton Abbey*, was virtually destroyed. The lifestyle of lavish parties and daily extravagances while the servants below stairs were paid a pittance were over. Girls were discovering that a whole new world lay at their feet.

However, the cotton industry was in serious trouble after the Great War. America, India and Japan had been slowly buying up British cotton manufacturing machinery and railway rolling stock since the 1880s and they had started their own cotton manufacturing industries. This resulted in undercutting on prices, loss of trade, and when Japan started twenty-four-hour working of their cotton mills in the early 1920s it meant that they could fulfil orders far more quickly and cheaply than in the UK. In 1930 the Cotton Board established the practice of choosing annual 'cotton queens': young, attractive, vibrant, cotton workers to travel and promote the industry and its products. However, it was too little, too late.

Those returning from the Great War had not found the promised 'land fit for heroes' but a land of high unemployment, acute housing shortage, food rationing and massive national debt. Women, who had been sole breadwinners, were thrown out of their jobs and replaced by men, leaving many with no means of supporting themselves. Any female resistance was often met with derision, sometimes a good beating and, occasionally, rape. Women certainly had a stronger political voice since being given the vote in 1918 and universal suffrage – that is the right to vote for all citizens in Britain aged 21 and over (the minimum voting age is now 18) except criminals and the insane – was granted in 1928. Mine-owners and mill-owners, desperate to retain their wealth, lowered workers' wages to try to maintain the status quo. Many had lost money by investing in war loans and bonds during the Great War, attracted by the promised high returns that, of course, the government could not meet. Unemployment doubled and there was much poverty and many food shortages. The Jarrow Hunger March of 1936 took place when 200 men from the Tyneside town of Jarrow marched to London asking for re-establishment of industry in the town after the closure of its shipyard. They were led by Ellen Wilkinson, the Mancunian who at that time was MP for Jarrow but who became Minister of Education just after the end of the Second World War.

The Home Front was resurrected in September 1938 during the Munich Crisis when Chamberlain was busy at the Munich Conference trying to negotiate with Hitler over the Sudetenland. Civilians had been encouraged to join either the Air Raid Precautions (ARP) or the Auxiliary Fire Service (AFS).

The ARP organization was a response to the common fear, instilled by the events of the Great War, of mass bombing from the air that had terrified millions of people. On 3 September 1939 Britain declared war on Germany and the women of Manchester were once again in the forefront of support for the Home Front. The declaration of this new war meant that female workers were initially once more at a premium. Women fulfilled roles of housewives, mothers, volunteers, helpers, etc. They were responsible for cooking, cleaning, washing, making or mending clothes for their families, bringing up the children, volunteering to help with the war effort, helping in air-raids or with evacuations, providing treats for the troops; the list was endless. In June 1939 the Women's Auxiliary Air Force (WAAF) had been established. Those who joined had to be aged 18 to 43. Initially the main working responsibilities involved driving, clerical tasks and cooking. Many women learned to drive during the Second World War as a matter of necessity. There was not enough time or resources for many lessons or for everyone to take a driving test, so women were taught the mechanics of driving a vehicle and the basic points of the Highway Code. In any case there was little motorized traffic on the roads due to costs and fuel rationing, and women drove cars and lorries as efficiently as the men; then, after the war, they simply carried on driving without taking any test.

Manchester waterways had long been an essential part of its transport network and whole families lived and worked on the canal boats. The canals were particularly important as a means of transport during the Second World War because they could save fuel and carry heavier loads than lorries. As more men were called up, many of the narrow boats or barges were worked quite efficiently by the women for the Inland Waterways, or I.W. as they were known. Never ones to miss an opportunity for sniggering, some working men quipped that I.W. really stood for Idle Women. In reality, the women were anything but idle. Narrow boats today are comparatively luxuriously equipped, mostly for tourist holidays. Seventy years ago the main job of the boats was to carry cargo. Living quarters and sleeping arrangements were extremely cramped, with the space for a family limited to one or two small rooms squashed up against the hold below deck. For more than 150 years women whose husbands worked the boats had cooked, washed, cleaned and brought up families in these conditions. Now, in addition, they had the men's work to do as well. Canal locks were frequent and often laborious to work, while steering the boats, especially either into locks or through tunnels, required considerable skill.

As the war progressed, jobs for women expanded rapidly into other areas such as maintaining barrage balloons and flying planes between British airfields. Barrage balloons – large oval silver-grey balloons, sometimes known as 'blimps' and tethered by metal cables – were used as a form of defence to try to force aircraft to fly at higher altitudes, making their approach more difficult and making it harder to hit intended targets. The balloons were deployed and maintained by members of the WAAF and a Mancunian lady named Irene Forsdyke was one of those chosen to work on the barrage balloons guarding Manchester. As she discovered, it was a task that needed careful concentration, conscientiousness and courage, plus a good deal of technical knowledge. Ten weeks' training was necessary and it was essential that the women understood the meaning of teamwork in case of serious problems with the balloons or adverse weather conditions. The balloons had a standard 90ft (27.5m) 'circle' and a winch powered by a Ford V8 engine to raise and lower them. The last few feet of the cable drum was painted red as a warning because if the metal cable ran off the drum the balloon would become loose and operators were in danger of being decapitated.

A week before Christmas in 1939 the British government passed the National Service (No.2) Act. All men and women aged 18 to 60 were now liable for national service which included military service for those under the age of 51. It was the first time women had been conscripted and also the first military registration of those aged 18. In Manchester women were called up to work in the munitions and aircraft manufacturing industries. Girls leaving school were given three choices: they could work in the factories, much of which involved war projects and making ammunitions; they could work on the land as a member of the Land Army; or they could train as a teacher. Many young women found these options disappointing but accepted that they had no choice. The author's mother chose teaching so that she would have a profession she could follow after the war had ended. Teaching young children had long been seen as 'women's work' and, while she chaffed at that description, the idea of helping to guide the young minds of future generations appealed to her. Anyone who told her she was just doing that job because she would get long holidays soon realized that they had made a serious error of judgement.

The Land Army, or the Land Girls as they were known, worked long hard hours for low wages in often poor conditions but most of them enjoyed the work and the camaraderie. Their uniform consisted of a green jumper, brown trousers, brown felt hats and a khaki overcoat, and their badge depicted a wheatsheaf that was symbolic of the work they did. Tasks included milking cows, lambing, looking after poultry, ploughing, harvesting, digging ditches, muck-spreading, cutting out foot-rot in sheep and applying Stockholm tar afterwards, or any other work required about the farms. A separate timber corps, known as lumber-jills, cut down trees, managed woodlands and operated sawmills.

Those employed in factories often worked on munitions and armaments, but they could find themselves doing a wide variety of jobs. One girl began by making haversacks for military personnel before being deployed to making light suits for soldiers and then working in an aircraft factory helping to manufacture turrets for the Lancaster bombers. Manchester had a thriving aircraft industry throughout the Second World War. The aircraft manufacturing company known as Avro was founded by Alliott Verdon Roe in 1910 at the Brownsfield Mill on Great Ancoats Street. Avro developed the Avro 679 Manchester at the beginning of the war, the forerunner of the much more successful four-engine Avro Lancaster, and they also had an experimental station at Ringway Airport (now Manchester International

Airport) on the edge of the city where the planes were tested. Women largely staffed the munitions factories, cotton mills, hat-works and catering establishments. Although women were conscripted into work in factories from 1942 onwards, the men were free with their complaints. Dinner would not be on the table when they returned home. The home was not kept as they would like it. Their children were being fed from tins and not being looked after or disciplined properly. Even worse, some women earned more than their husbands and, in men's eyes, this was shameful indeed. The resulting exhaustion and stress suffered by many women was hardly noticed. Munitions work could be difficult and dangerous. The girls who worked in the munitions factories were known as the 'canary girls', exactly as they had been in the Great War, because constant contact with the chemicals involved turned their skin yellow. While some women's hair might turn blonde because of the exposure to chemicals, natural blondes sometimes found their hair turning green.

There was (and still is) a belief that the only real work is paid work. This ignores the fact that much, if not most, of the work done in Britain during the war was unpaid and done mainly by women. Women fulfilled the roles of housewives, mothers, volunteers, helpers, etc. They were responsible for cooking, cleaning, washing, making or mending clothes for their families, bringing up the children, volunteering to help with the war effort, helping in air-raids or with evacuations, providing treats for the troops; the list was endless, and all the jobs were unpaid. If a woman had children under 14 (then the school leaving age) at home, she was not required to work outside the home at a paid 'day job'. However, the contributions made by these women were not only valuable but essential to the smooth running and mobilization of the country and its fighting force. Even if they did do any paid or voluntary work, their domestic responsibilities remained central to their lives. Many women in Manchester took paid work as a necessity rather than a choice, whatever their status. They might take in washing or offer dressmaking and childcare facilities, jobs that could be done in the home, to earn a little extra to meet the ever-rising costs of living. Those who couldn't do so frequently felt guilty. Britain was the most completely mobilized country in the Second World War. A third of the population was engaged in war work and aircraft production trebled. However, although women filled jobs in industry, services and business, much as they had done during the Great War, they still had to contend with low wages, long hours and opposition from men.

Fire-watching in Manchester was done by civil defence volunteers, many of them women. The tallest buildings had small shelters that could accommodate fire-watchers and their job was to see where the incendiary bombs fell, then take appropriate action. The author's mother was one of the fire-watchers in the city. She worked as a teacher at an infants' school in Ardwick during the day, while at night she had rostered fire-watching duties. Often lonely, cold and scared, she would watch the bombs dropping and desperately pray that they would not hit the building where she was on fire-watching duty. She was one of the lucky ones. It was dangerous work and numbers of fire-fighters lost their lives.

The roles of official voluntary occupations were also incredibly important. The two main volunteer organizations were the Air Raid Precautions (ARP) and the Women's Voluntary Service (WVS). The ARP, which had both male and female members, organized public air-raid shelters and ensured that blackout regulations were kept. The ARP also helped in the aftermath of air-raids, searching for survivors and giving first-aid to casualties. The WVS made bandages, knitted or sewed clothing and comforts for the troops, and ran canteens at ports and railway stations for members of the armed forces. Jobs could range from the cleaning of children's gas masks to collecting salvage to cooking meals and arranging housing for those who lost their homes in air-raids. In Manchester they assisted with the evacuation of the city's schoolchildren and the children evacuated from Guernsey to Manchester. The WVS has sometimes been referred to as 'the army that Hitler forgot.'

An unexpected casualty of the Second World War in Manchester was the ice cream industry. On 10 June 1940 Italy, under the leadership of Benito Mussolini, had entered the war on the side of Germany. This had a devastating effect on 'Little Italy', the Italian quarter of Manchester centred on Ancoats, a residential area bordering the city centre. There had been a sizeable number of Italians in Manchester since the latter half of the nineteenth century when thousands of Italian workers left the farming regions of Italy in search of work, and an Italian colony clustered together and settled in Ancoats. As the cotton industry began to decline the Italians had turned to the skills of making ice cream which they had brought from their homeland. Italian ice cream, then as now, proved very popular. Ben's and Granelli's ice creams started life in Ancoats; their vendors were described as 'friendly and colourful'. The Italians were sociable people and integrated well with their English neighbours. Some Italians married English girls and took on British citizenship. Numbers of them had served in the Great War with the British forces so it came as a great shock to discover that suddenly they were the enemy. Whereas before there had been only welcome and friendliness, there were now riots against the 'Italian enemies'. Churchill saw them all as a national security threat and ordered internment of every Italian male aged between 17 and 60. The men were arrested and taken away, leaving their wives and children in tears without any form of support and ice cream manufacture was banned (although mainly due to a shortage of raw materials rather than the fact that it was an Italian industry). Community activities involving Italians were also banned and a curfew was imposed. It was a miserable time for Italian families and in addition they had to suffer rampant dislike and distrust from people they had previously considered their friends. Italian women found the disruption and dislocation particularly hard. Not only did they lose their menfolk but their children were evacuated, and many were left feeling totally bereft. Manchester, however, was much kinder to its Italian population than the neighbouring city of Liverpool or other towns and cities in the United Kingdom where there were riots and Italian businesses were attacked and destroyed. Although Ancoats folk did not show much active hostility towards their Italian neighbours, the community changed and some Italians left Manchester for good.

Lancashire cotton goods still had an excellent reputation for quality worldwide, but the cotton trade in Manchester was suffering and cotton manufacturers had been keen to emphasize the importance of the export trade in wartime. There were problems, however, involving pressures of demand, shortage of supplies, rising prices, dislocation of workers, delivery difficulties and trade outlets and, as the year progressed, cotton exports continued to fall. The Cotton Board wanted to institute a five-year plan for future development and success, but this relied on government support and the question of wages. The Lancashire cotton trade could not compete on wage levels with other parts of the world where very low wages were paid, but the Cotton Board was anxious to resolve that discrepancy by the volume of export trade and differential pricing rather than controlled pricing. Female workers in the city still had to earn what they could, when and where they could. Married women continued to experience problems with their earnings. One example was the question of post-war tax credits for wives which had only partially been resolved. The Chancellor said that the certificate was usually issued to the husband when some other tax-related form or notice was being sent to him. Notice of assessment in respect of a wife's earnings was not sent to her but to her husband. There were audible murmurings of discontent and it was hastily added:

> under a new arrangement which is now being introduced…at the same time as the notice is sent to the husband the wife will be sent a separate notification, either at her home address, if known, or at her place of employment, notifying her that the certificate for the previous year is being issued.

This would explain her rights and stated that where husband and wife agreed apportionment the credit would be divided accordingly. This arrangement would only apply to wives who were in employment and paying tax that was deducted from their wages. However, it could not be guaranteed that the notification to the wife would be sent at the same time as the certificate went to the husband. Mancunian women were not impressed, and many felt that their husbands still controlled their earnings, even after all the struggle and legislation.

However, on 6 August 1946 the Family Allowances Act came into operation, awarding mothers a tax-free cash payment for each child after the eldest. It was the first time in Britain that a payment from the state had been given directly to women. Despite this, a number of wives felt they still needed to have their husband's permission to go out to work. Social expectations die hard. After the Second World War and throughout the 1950s, it remained the usual expectation that when a girl married she would give up her job and stay at home to look after her husband and her family. Peer pressure ensured that this was often the case and most women were expected to defer to their husbands in many matters. Thus the image of the 'little woman' was perpetuated and officials such as bank managers and lawyers could be very patronizing, with some refusing to do business unless the husband was present. This situation continued until the 1970s when the fight for feminine equality reached new heights after Germaine Greer published her book *The Female Eunuch* and 'Women's Lib' became the new battle-cry.

CHAPTER THREE

Aspects of Women's Lives in Home and Romance: Courtship, Marriage, Divorce, Housing, Food, Clothes, Pregnancy

During the nineteenth century, as in several preceding centuries, unmarried women were seen as a prize to be pursued and wooed, treated chivalrously and sometimes fought over in the rituals that led up to a wedding and the long walk down the aisle. However, once the wedding ring was on her finger, a woman lost her independence, her property, her basic civil rights and even any control over her own body. For many life was little better than that of a slave and sometimes a great deal worse. As more than one Manchester cynic put it, marriage was simply a form of legalized prostitution crossed with slavery. A wife was required to allow her husband conjugal rights whenever he demanded them. Her feelings or physical comfort were simply not an issue. Even if she was ill, in pain, recovering from childbirth or sore from beatings, it was irrelevant. She had no rights over her own body which now belonged to her husband. She had no rights over her own possessions either. Literally everything she owned, even herself, became her husband's property upon marriage. If she had any income, whether earned or from a trust, it automatically belonged to her husband after the wedding. She could not spend any money without his permission. She could not leave the house without his permission. She could not entertain friends or family without his permission. Her husband's word was absolute law at all times in all matters.

Women who resisted this harsh and unfair state of affairs suffered badly. Working-class women would usually be beaten and frequently quite badly injured. Upper-class women were threatened with losing their children or being locked away in a sanatorium for the insane. In 1848 Anne Brontë, whose sister, Charlotte, was friendly with the Manchester novelist Elizabeth Gaskell, summed up the feelings of many women in her novel *The Tenant of Wildfell Hall* when she wrote 'that though in single life your joys may not be very many, your sorrows, at least, will not be more than you can bear.' Coventry Patmore, a well-known Victorian poet, wrote *The Angel in the House* in 1854 in which he declared that 'the perfect wife had to put her husband's happiness first in everything' and that 'she should worship him after death, sacrificing her own happiness to preserve his memory.' 'The Angel in the House' had to be 'passive, self-sacrificing, meek, submissive, charming, pious, full of selfless devotion, sympathetic, devoid of any power of her own, and chastely pure.' To modern eyes (2018) this is crying for the moon but in nineteenth-century England many men expected precisely these virtues in their wives, no matter how badly they treated them. If a woman did not conform to the ideals of this fictional paragon, who was not expected to have any emotions or needs of her own, they were made to feel they were failures. It is little wonder that in Victorian England many women who could do so took to their beds as invalids. Only in that way could they escape and get some attention for themselves. During the first two decades of Queen Victoria's reign (1837–57), the scandal of the upper-class George Norton's treatment of his wife, Caroline, became a cause célèbre, and she wrote many letters to the queen pleading her case. She made a number of valid points concerning the injustices meted out to women which included:

1. '...a married woman has no legal existence in England...[and] she has no possessions...'
2. '...an English wife cannot make a will...the law gives what she has to her husband...'
3. '...an English wife cannot legally claim her own earnings...'
4. '...an English wife may not leave her husband's house...' (i.e. leave home)
5. '...if her husband takes proceedings for divorce she is not allowed to defend herself...'
6. '...if an English wife is guilty of infidelity her husband can divorce her...but she cannot divorce her husband (for the same reason)'
7. '...she cannot prosecute for libel...'
8. '...she cannot sign a lease, or transact responsible business...'

Finally, at the instigation of the queen, the Divorce and Matrimonial Causes Act was amended in 1857, and although it still contained many inequalities, there was a new and important clause enabling deserted wives to keep their own earnings. A further Matrimonial Causes Act was passed in 1878 allowing women to seek a judicial separation from violent husbands, but any real sense of equality in the divorce courts was not achieved until 1923. However, it was still difficult and expensive for women to divorce, and there was also a stigma attached to lone divorced women even when they were not the party at fault; a situation that lasted until the 1970s. As one upset and irritated Manchester woman put it:

> He wanted to have his cake and eat it so when I refused to share a house with his mistress he claimed that I was being difficult and that the divorce was my luxury. We divorced in the early 1960s and almost at once I became a kind of social outcast. Women distrusted me and their husbands usually assumed I was simply desperate for sex. I learned quickly, if I was invited to any social gathering, to always leave alone and go home alone. His life wasn't affected and yet he was the guilty party.

The outcry over the discrimination against women was far more vociferous in the north of England in general, and in Manchester in particular, because of the large numbers of women working in the mills and manufactories in appalling conditions, often for paltry wages, and living in conditions that most upper-class folk would not have inflicted upon a dog they didn't like. Women worked up to twelve hours a day in the mills but their earnings did not belong to them. Their husbands could take every penny without so much as a by-your-leave. When a man finished work for the day he could either sit at home with his newspaper and relax or, as was more usual, go to the pub spending his, and frequently his wife's, hard-earned cash on drink. When a woman finished work for the day she had to go home to clean, cook and care for her children. Many lived in the infamous 'courts' in Manchester (apartment blocks built around a courtyard) with sometimes as many as 300 folk sharing scant sanitation facilities.

Some families lived in one room in damp basements. Tucked into an 'oxbow' on the River Medlock near the present Oxford Road railway station was the area known as 'Little Ireland' due to the large number of Irish immigrants who lived there. Many had emigrated as a result of the Irish potato famine in the 1840s/50s. Engels described Little Ireland as:

> '...about 200 cottages, built chiefly back-to-back, in which live about 4,000 human beings...the cottages are old, dirty, and of the smallest sort, the streets uneven, fallen into ruts and in part without drains or pavement; masses of refuse, offal, and sickening filth lie among standing pools in all directions...' and he went on to say how '....a horde of ragged women and children swarm about here, filthy as the swine that thrive upon the garbage heaps and in the puddles...'

Overcrowding was rife. Disease was rife. Cholera, typhoid and TB were rife. Infant mortality was as high as four in ten in some areas. Anyone who could afford to do so lived as far from the mills as they could. Slum clearance actually began in

Manchester during the 1850s, but many of the grim little back-to-backs, one-up-one-down and two-up-two-down cottages survived well into the twentieth century.

From the early 1870s to the late 1890s the Manchester slums suffered additionally from a new phenomenon known as 'scuttlers'. These were gangs of young working-class males, usually aged from 12 or 13 to 18 or 19 whose main aim seemed to be fighting other similar gangs, the basis for which appeared to be territorial. They were prevalent in the inner-city suburbs of Ancoats, Bradford, Miles Platting, Openshaw and neighbouring Gorton. Gang members usually wore a 'uniform' of brass-tipped clogs, bell-bottomed trousers, heavy buckled belts and 'flashy scarves', and they carried knives. Hair was cut short at the back and sides but with a fringe longer on the left side over which peaked caps were worn, tilted to the left to show the fringe. *Peaky Blinders*, shown on television in 2017 and 2018, was named after a Birmingham scuttling gang that took its name from these peaked caps which had the added refinement of razor blades sown into the cap peaks so that head-butting became a rather hazardous business. Generally, however, fewer and lighter injuries were inflicted with knives than in twenty-first-century gang warfare and there were very few deaths. Frightening they might have been, but the gangs attacked each other rather than women and children. There were hardly any female gangs in Manchester but it became a badge of honour to be the girlfriend of a scuttler and they wore distinctive vertically-striped skirts. For both boys and girls the scuttling gangs were a kind of status symbol. By 1900 the gangs were fast becoming a thing of the past because of much slum demolition and the establishment of 'Working Lads' Clubs' and local football clubs to divert the attention of young men from mischief-making and fighting. It was not considered necessary to provide any such alternatives for girls.

Due to the poverty of the interwar years (1919–39), some of these cramped dwellings remained in use until the slum clearances of the 1950s and 1960s. In the outer leafier suburbs of the city there was some house-building during the 1920s and

1930s but these homes were of a style and size that only the better-off folk could afford. When the back-to-backs and 'courts' were finally demolished they were often replaced by tall blocks of flats rather than individual homes. Although by comparison the new flats were light and airy and had all 'mod cons' (such as running water and inside toilets), the sense of community somehow virtually disappeared. Folk could no longer sit out on their doorsteps, having a good gossip with each other. Gardens were rare. There was little, if any, space for children to go out and play. Residents no longer knew who their neighbours were. The material improvement of living conditions had come at a cost.

Pleas for higher wages and better living conditions were met with the usual response that industry could not afford it. Malnourishment was common among the poorer classes of Manchester in the second half of the nineteenth century when porridge, bread and potatoes formed the staple diet. There would be porridge for breakfast, with bread and cheese or dripping for lunch (often just a hunk of bread for poorer families), while potato pie (sometimes made from potato peelings in the Second World War), potato rissoles, potato fritters, potatoes boiled, mashed, baked or fried, were all common suppertime meals in the millscapes. Irish colcannon made from potatoes, onions, cabbage and, if they could afford it, a bit of bacon, was very popular. Cow heels were also cheap and popular. They were mostly either boiled or fried, or made into soup with a few potatoes and other vegetables. Pigs' trotters could be boiled or roasted. Sweetbreads, a kind of offal dish made from the thymus or pancreas, usually of calf or lamb, were regularly enjoyed and so too were calf brains. A traditional Friday night treat for Manchester citizens was tripe, the stomach lining of a cow or sheep, served hot or cold with onions. Aborted calf foetuses provided a 'Sunday roast' for the poorest people. Meat auctions were often held in the city pubs on Saturday nights, and seasonal vegetables could be bought fairly cheaply from the Saturday-night markets that went on until late in the evening. Rickets and vitamin deficiencies were common, however, since many of the poorer families could not often afford a well-balanced diet.

During the Great War David Lloyd George made repeated requests for wealthier folk to buy the better cuts of meat and leave the cheaper cuts for poorer folk. This fell on deaf ears, as did other requests to cut back on certain foodstuffs. Food rationing, which began in early 1918, actually evened out the gap in good nutrition between rich and poor by ensuring that everyone got some of everything at a reasonable price and this, to everyone's astonishment, actually eradicated the diseases of malnutrition such as rickets, scurvy, vitamin deficiencies, stunted growth, etc. However, before compulsory rationing was introduced the government came up with some almost unpalatable suggestions. There were fried porridge scones – an echo of the stiff onion-flavoured porridge slices fed to children working in the mills of the nineteenth century so that they could eat with one hand and continue working at their tasks with the other hand – minced celery fritters, and the jewel in the crown was an alternative to a second or third vegetable. Housewives and cooks were advised to boil potato peelings with stale bread and old vegetable leaves and then mash them through a sieve into a brown purée to be served with meat and potatoes.

During the interwar years, when rationing ceased and unemployment increased, nutritional levels declined again and numbers of children went hungry. Schools provided some food for their pupils but the school holidays were a lean time for many. There were hunger marches throughout the 1920s and 1930s, culminating in the Jarrow Hunger March of October 1936. In 1931 a means test had been imposed on unemployment benefits which had made matters even worse. Ellen Wilkinson, a Manchester-born-and-bred woman with a reputation for being a 'firebrand', was the Labour MP for Jarrow at that time and she led the march which took almost four weeks to complete. There was a great deal of general sympathy but little practical help offered. Meanwhile, back in Manchester, mothers still struggled to cope and children continued to go to bed hungry. Food rationing was reintroduced at the beginning of the Second World War which improved the situation a little again, although quantities of foods allowed were often sparse, more so than in the Great War. Like their counterparts everywhere, Manchester women bore the main brunt of the quest for economy and conservation of food supplies. Although some worked on the allotments, it was their role in the kitchen that was most important. A leaflet entitled 'Women and the Home Front' openly exhorted women to refrain from hoarding or encouraging profiteering and to take pride in daily thrift because, said the leaflet, '...in this spirit, we can fight to conquer...the greed and selfishness which are the ultimate causes of war itself...'.

Recipes of the Second World War centre heavily on fruit and vegetables and meat-free main dishes were popular. A variation on the modern quiche lorraine was a flan of potatoes, onions, celery and a little cheese mixed in a white sauce and baked in a pastry flan case. Rice puddings made with water (the taste is indistinguishable from those made with milk) were very popular, and so were suet-based puddings like jam roly-poly or spotted dick. The water from boiled cabbages was said to make a refreshing drink. Fish and chip shops were popular, although fish was often in short supply and expensive. Churchill was also very keen on Lloyd George's idea of national kitchens which had proved a great success in the First World War, and the idea was revived early in 1940. Initially they were called community kitchens until Churchill renamed them British Kitchens or Restaurants. The concept was just the same as in the Great War. The kitchens could bulk-buy fresh foods at cost and cook cheap nourishing meals on a small number of industrial cookers. This saved money on individual food purchases and the fuel for running individual cookers. Customers could buy a meat and two veg main course followed by a pudding for the modern equivalent of £1. Meals would be simple but quite palatable: spam (a small tinned luncheon meat loaf made from bacon and ham) with mashed potato, hotpot, stew, pie and mash, baked potatoes, curry (of anything; curried carrots were a favoured dish) and rice, greens in season, with maybe a rice or suet pudding to follow. Horsemeat was also used and there was a horsemeat butchers in Gorton. There would be soup as well, but usually a thin vegetable broth, not the thick soups folk have become used to today. Manchester had a number of British Restaurants, staffed and run by women, which proved ideal for those working long hours, busy mothers trying to be both breadwinners and home-makers as well as caring for their children, and those with limited budgets or cooking facilities.

There was a great shortage of eggs and only one fresh egg per person per week was allowed. This included eggs used in cooking (i.e. cakes, puddings, etc). To fill the gap, dried egg was imported from America and was almost universally disliked. Used in cooking other dishes its taste could be disguised but many folk considered it unpalatable when eaten on its own. One young Manchester woman, who became pregnant in the late autumn of 1946, said the best thing about her pregnancy was that she was allowed four fresh eggs a week instead of one. The Second World War ended in 1945 but not the food shortages, and rationing in some form continued until 1954. Offal remained popular because it was cheap and nutritious. Liver and onions in a good gravy were a common dish, although the cheaper ox liver was much tougher than lamb's liver. Herrings, a very bony fish, were also plentiful and liked for the same reasons of economy. Kippers (smoked herrings) were a common breakfast dish in Manchester and also in seaside lodging houses where Manchester folk stayed during the Wakes weeks. There were neither the supermarkets nor the wide range of imported foods available today, so Manchester folk had to be content with whatever happened to be naturally in season. In winter this meant potatoes, kale, cabbage, sprouts, parsnips and turnips, and the only fresh fruits were apples or pears. Oranges were very popular and widely sought-after but during and after the Second World War they were very scarce.

The burden of cooking always fell to the women. Victorian men regarded the kitchen as an exclusively female domain. Before the Great War there were very few 'mod cons' or convenience foods. Domestic chores in the nineteenth century, and before the Great War in the twentieth century, were hard and unremitting for women. Floors were swept and washed by hand. The washing of clothes, bedding, towels and curtains was all done by hand in the nineteenth century using dolly tubs (for a warm wash), coppers (for a boil wash) and washboards for scrubbing. Most kitchen activities were also done by hand and most cooking was done from scratch. There were no microwave ovens, few blenders or mixers, and domestic refrigerators were not common before the 1920s. Washing machines were rare and dishwashers almost unknown until the 1960s. Victorian women cooked on a range or over a coal fire. Early twentieth-century women had gas cookers and, later, electric cookers. Soups, stocks, gravies and custards etc. were made at home and did not come out of packets or tins. Pies, cakes, biscuits, tarts and puddings were also mostly home-made. There were no supermarkets, so different groceries and household items had to be bought from different shops, making the weekly shop a time-consuming affair. Hence in many households particular days of the week were allotted to particular tasks. For example, washing was done on Mondays, ironing on Tuesdays, cleaning on Wednesdays, shopping on Thursdays and baking on Fridays. However, for women working twelve-hour days in the mills this was simply not an option and tasks were undertaken as and when possible. The idea of men helping out with domestic chores or being 'house-husbands' belongs to the latter part of the twentieth century, while the idea of the 'little woman' at home in the kitchen persisted into the 1950s and early 1960s. Usually advertisements for any household products would show a smiling female neatly dressed in a skirt and apron using the recommended item to improve her already pristine home. The home was, and often still is, seen as the woman's domain.

Feminine clothing and fashions underwent a complete revolution between 1850 and 1950. The phrase 'from the sublime to the ridiculous' needs to be inverted to 'from the ridiculous to the sublime' to sum up the changes in women's clothing during this period. In 1850 the crinoline was all the rage. This was a huge unwieldy underskirt over a frame made originally from horsehair (crin) and linen or cotton – later from steel, whalebone, cane or rubber – to give the overskirt a 'hoop appearance'. Pleasing to men they may have been, but the crinoline skirts were incredibly dangerous. They got caught up in machinery (especially in the mills) or carriage wheels, with often disastrous results; caused women to fall from trains and horse buses; or caught fire if a woman was too near an open hearth. There were any number of obstacles that caused problems for crinoline-wearers, and hundreds of women were injured or even died through crinoline accidents in Britain. The Duchess of Manchester suffered a 'crinoline accident' in 1859 although, fortunately for her, it was merely embarrassing rather than injurious. She was attempting to cross a stile and moved too quickly. 'The Duchess caught a hoop of her cage in it,' wrote Eleanor Stanley, 'and went regularly head over heels with her cage and petticoats above her head.' However, to the Victorian onlookers the most shocking thing about this incident was it revealed that the Duchess was 'wearing a pair of scarlet tartan knickerbockers'. In polite Victorian society, undergarments were simply never even mentioned, let alone seen.

By the 1870s the crinoline had been largely replaced by the bustle, a much smaller framework, worn at the back, just below the waist, to try and keep skirts from dragging. Female dress continued to remain restrictive and often uncomfortable, however, and in 1881 the Rational Dress Society was founded in London. Its manifesto declared that it was a protest against 'the wearing of tightly fitting corsets, of high heeled shoes, of heavily weighted skirts...all tie down cloaks...impeding movement of the arms...crinolines or crinolettes...' Garments 'should be suspended from the shoulders, not the hips, which renders the wearing of corsets unnecessary.' These aims appealed to large numbers of women, especially those working in the mills of Manchester. Whalebone corsets were often excruciatingly uncomfortable and the lower point would dig painfully into the legs, bruising them, every time the wearer bent over. The author wore a whalebone corset dating from c.1914 for three days as part of a costume pageant and the resulting bruises took more than three weeks to heal. Looser forms of underwear, like camisoles, chemises and shifts, were much more comfortable and far healthier to wear. Men, however, who did not have to suffer such indignities, were not impressed by the aims of the Rational Dress Society. It was 'an American thing' like Amelia Bloomer's 'divided skirts' (i.e. bloomers or waist-to-ankle-length knickers rather in the style of Turkish harem pants). The thought of English women wearing such things led to accusations that similar garments had been worn during the French Revolution and that 'such attire would necessarily lead to unrest and possibly violence.' The hysteria that had been caused by Welsh female miners wearing 'divided skirts' (i.e. trousers) for reasons of safety and ease of movement in restricted areas had led to groups of 'horrified' young men going to watch them, voyeurism seeking thrills, while pretending to assess the 'risks to femininity'. There were no female miners in the Manchester coal mines but the female cotton mill workers would have been infinitely more comfortable and much safer at work than having to drag swirling skirts around.

Girls were generally dressed in the same style as their mothers but wore shorter skirts, and the ubiquitous red flannel petticoats for warmth and modesty, until they reached puberty and, until around 1920, boys also wore short dresses until the age of 4 or 5. The Great War and the winning of the vote for women had finally put paid to restrictive clothing and full-length skirts as obligatory wear for females. The fashion during the 1920s was for loose low-waisted dresses.

By the 1930s, blouses and the upper part of dresses had become more shapely but skirts were still loose and calf-length. School uniforms for older girls had now become established. Most secondary school uniforms consisted of a long-sleeved white blouse or top and a gymslip often in black, navy blue or grey. Gymslips were a pinafore style of tunic that hung from the shoulder to below the knees, usually with a self-coloured belt or sash at the waist.

Many schools also had a summer uniform which allowed the girls to wear a short-sleeved, below knee-length dress, usually made from red, blue or green gingham check material. The huge fashion 'scandal' (to men at least) of the 1920s and 1930s was the advent and popularity of trousers for females.

Trousers were frequently more practical, safer, warmer and easier to wear, and for females doing war work as mechanics or pilots (in the Second World War) or as Land Army girls, they were essential. Working trousers for women were straight like men's trousers but for evening wear the wider pantaloon style was popular and made respectable by film actresses such as Marlene Dietrich and Katharine Hepburn. Even in the twenty-first century, certain dress codes make it clear that trousers for women are frowned upon, but female trouser-wearing has been around a long time. There is a depiction on a Greek vase, dating from around 470BC, of an Amazon lady wearing trousers and a tunic that would not be out of place as a twenty-first-century fashion statement.

The need to conserve supplies in the Second World War brought in the introduction of utility clothing: skirts, tops, dresses and undergarments were to be made using the minimum of materials and skirts were to be just below knee-length. The Board of Trade had sponsored several ranges of 'utility clothing' for the war that had strict specifications on the amounts of material to be used and the labour involved. No turn-ups were allowed on trousers, nor were double-breasted suits allowed. Skirt and coat lengths were regulated. All utility clothing carried the label 'CC41' with 'CC' standing for Controlled Commodity and '41' referring to the year in which this measure had been instigated. Leading fashion designers such as Norman Hartnell and Hardy Amies were commissioned to design clothing for the utility ranges and maximum prices chargeable for both cloth and clothing were laid down. Women became adept at 'make do and mend' by using old clothes and curtains to make new items of wear or by adorning faded clothes with bits of lace or ribbon, a bow, or perhaps a frill added to the skirt. For many Manchester women this was second nature because of their employment in the textile mills. Some items, such as silk or nylon stockings, were difficult if not impossible to obtain. Many girls and women either wore ankle socks or nothing with their shoes. Most nylon stockings still had vertical back seams and those wanting to dress up and look chic emulated these stocking seams by drawing them down their legs with eyeliner pencils or charcoal. Lines of 'national footwear' were also produced, although the height of heels was strictly limited. Despite a brief return during the 1950s to the fashion looks of the 1930s it did not last and the 1960s brought the advent of jeans and the mini-skirt. Female fashions would never be the same again.

A uniquely feminine issue down the ages is that of menstruation. Most men simply didn't want to know about such matters and most women were mortified by even the thought of discussing such a subject with them. It was a social taboo and it was often viewed as 'unclean', especially by the church, despite the fact that it is a perfectly natural function in healthy women of child-bearing age. More important for women were the practical problems it posed. For late-twentieth-century women, daily baths or showers and disposable sanitary wear took much of the hassle away, but for their counterparts of the nineteenth century, especially in the poverty-stricken, cramped and often dirty surroundings of their home life in industrial Manchester, menstruation was a difficult time. In earlier centuries women had used ragged off-cuts or strips of absorbent cloth (hence the common term of 'rags' to describe sanitary wear) to soak up the blood and had then washed them out ready for the next time. Others, however, especially the very poor, simply bled into their clothes. It was not uncommon for women to bleed into a chemise that they would then wear for seven or eight days at least. In areas of industrial Manchester close to the mills with a severe lack of facilities, many working-class women would have had neither the time, the space, nor even the clean running water for washing to do otherwise. At the very least the practice was totally unhygienic and liable to lead to infection. In the late 1870s, a sanitary belt was produced to be worn around the waist with washable pads attached. It was known as the Hoosier sanitary belt and forms of it persisted until the 1970s, although by that time the pads were disposable. Lister's towels, the first disposable sanitary towels, were manufactured by Johnson & Johnson in 1888 and the first tampon was invented in 1929, but poorer women would probably have been unable to afford them. Today (2018) there are still issues surrounding cost. Great controversy has been caused by the fact that sanitary protection is not seen as 'a necessity of life' and therefore is not exempt from Value Added Tax (VAT). The argument put forward is that most females don't even use a single box of tampons each month and they cost so little that the VAT is minimal. The real problem lies in this generalization. There is great variation. Some women have light periods and may only use a dozen or so tampons, whereas some women's periods are so heavy they soak a pack of maternity-sized towels within twenty-four hours. Falling wages and rising costs may have an effect as well. The fact remains, however, that women must still pay extra tax for a natural function that they cannot avoid.

For Manchester women, abortion or adoption were not really viable alternatives to pregnancy due to the expense, danger and illegality of abortion and the lack of demand for babies to adopt because there were already numbers of 'excess' children. The major innovation that gave women greater freedom and more choice in their lives was access to birth control. The pioneering work of introducing birth-control clinics – although initially only married women could obtain contraception – was undertaken by a lady named Marie Stopes. She had received a PhD in botany from the University of Munich in 1904 and in that same year she took up the post of lecturer in palaeobotany at the University of Manchester (becoming the first female academic at Manchester), a post she held until 1910. During her time at the university she studied coal and Glossopteris (a type of seed fern). After a brief unhappy first marriage she married Humphrey Verdon Roe, a Manchester man and a member of the Manchester-based, family-run aircraft manufacturing company A.V. Roe (Avro). After her book *Married Love* (which clearly explained, for the first time in print, the processes of ovulation, menstruation, sexual intercourse and contraception) was published in 1918, Marie Stopes became interested in the idea of 'mothers' clinics' (birth-control clinics). She wanted to open the first one attached to St Mary's Hospital in Manchester, but the hospital declined her offer. Eventually she opened her first birth-control clinic in London in 1921 but returned to Manchester later to try and help to set up a further series of birth-control clinics.

Contraception would only be supplied to married women. It was still illegal for unmarried women to have access to contraception, although illegitimacy carried a strong social stigma for both mother and child. Availability of contraception for all women would only come with the Brook Clinics of the 1960s. Women flocked to the 'mothers' clinics', especially working-class women who already had a number of children and were struggling to care for them properly. Their husbands were not quite so enthusiastic. Elsie Plant was a young Manchester mother of three girls who believed strongly in equality for women. Her two eldest daughters had been born in 1913 and 1915 respectively and she had thought her family was complete, but late in 1921 she found herself pregnant for a third time. Elsie was more fortunate than many in that her husband ran his own business, which was doing well, but she had not wanted a third child. Her third daughter was born in the spring of 1922 and in 1923 Elsie tried to open a birth-control clinic in Stockport. However, at this time she found it impossible, partly due to opposition from the Catholic Church. Elsie and her husband were both prominent members of Stockport Labour Fellowship and through this organization they traced Marie Stopes, who was now living in London, and invited her to speak in Stockport which today forms part of Greater Manchester. The two women became friends and Elsie arranged several speaking engagements for her in the Manchester area. Nevertheless, Elsie was not successful in founding a local birth-control clinic until after the Second World War, although by that time it was under the auspices of the Family Planning Association (FPA) and not Marie Stopes. Elsie worked regularly in the FPA clinic for more than two decades, but she never forgot one of her experiences in the early years of its formation. She was confronted one day in the clinic by a very angry husband who demanded to know why she was trying to deny his virility. Elsie was taken aback. She explained carefully to him that, since his wife already had five children, his virility was not in doubt but they did not have the means to support more children. He lowered his face to hers and roared that she did not understand. He had to keep his wife pregnant or 'she went peculiar!' Marie Stopes herself also encountered a great deal of similar resistance but she too had persevered and gained admiration in many quarters for the independence and opportunities that she was creating for women to make their own choices.

There were, however, other reasons for Marie Stopes promoting birth control that had nothing to do with philanthropy, promoting female welfare or helping women to achieve greater measures of choice and independence by limiting the size of their families. She believed in and supported the ideals of eugenics. The Oxford English Dictionary defines eugenics as 'the science of improving a population by controlled breeding to increase the occurrence of desirable heritable characteristics.' Eugenics is the twin sister of genetic engineering. Marie Stopes was keen on 'purity of the race' and she advocated 'enforceable sterilisation of any man or woman deemed unfit to have children.' She criticized 'the diseased, the racially negligent, the thriftless, the careless, the feeble-minded, the very lowest and worst members of the community who...produced stunted, warped and inferior infants' and she had absolutely no time at all for those suffering from physical infirmity such as blindness, deafness, dumbness or mental health problems on any level, condemning them as 'wasteful eaters' (i.e. consuming food supplies she felt could be put to better use). She would later disinherit her only son for marrying a girl who was short-sighted and of whom she wrote:

> She has an inherited disease of the eyes which not only makes her wear hideous glasses so that it is horrid to look at her, but the awful curse will carry on and I have the horror of our line being so contaminated and little children with the misery of glasses... Mary and Harry are quite callous about both the wrong to their children, the wrong to my family and the eugenic crime.

Her words echoed those of the Nazi aims of a 'pure Aryan race'. Blue eyes, so prized as part of the Aryan ideal, are in fact a genetic mutation that occurred in the aftermath of widespread migration from Anatolia (south-eastern Turkey) and the shores of the Black Sea around 10,000 years ago. The 'pure' genetic eye colour of the human race was originally brown and it is still the prevalent eye colour of Mediterranean communities and countries of the East and of Africa. In 1935, at around the same time as her second marriage began to break down, Marie Stopes attended the Nazi Congress for Population Science in Germany. Like Hitler, she had an instinctive dislike of Jews (whom she declined to have in her home), gypsies and Russians. Yet she saw herself as patriotic when the Second World War broke out, becoming a Land Army girl and volunteering for fire-watching duties. However, in 1939 she had written to Hitler, enclosing a copy of her book *Love Songs for Young Lovers* for him to read, and in 1942 she penned a brief verse that she thought he would find particularly amusing:

> *'Catholics, Prussians, the Jews and the Russians,*
> *all are a curse or something worse.'*

The Museum of Terror in Berlin, which chronicles the historical events of Nazi Germany during the Second World War, and the exhibitions on display at the concentration camps of Auschwitz-Birkenau in Poland, carry reproductions of quotes and opinions from various leading SS men who dealt with Hitler's 'final solution' and ran the camps, from Adolf Eichmann who was ultimately responsible for mass exterminations, and from others involved in the promotion of the Aryan ideal, that are similar to the eugenic views promoted by Marie Stopes. It was discrimination carried to an ultimate logical conclusion and the human suffering it entailed is now a matter of history, anguish, discussion and the need to try to explain how such a thing as the Holocaust could have happened. Elsie, however, was simply a committed Socialist and suffragette who saw birth control as a means of allowing women some influence over the size of their families, thereby playing an important part in their growing attempts to achieve equality, choices and independence. Manchester also looked on the positive side of birth control as limiting the number of mouths that any one family needed to feed, thereby hopefully increasing the standard of living for everyone. There are still clinics in the city named after Marie Stopes, but today their main aim is to prevent unwanted pregnancy for any woman who finds herself in a situation where pregnancy would be disastrous on a personal level for both her and her family, not to rid the world of all the infinite variations of man and womankind or the contributions each different group can make to the development of the human race.

CHAPTER FOUR

Health:
Local Public Health Reports, Maternity Pre-NHS, Sexual Health, Effects of Poverty on Health, Mental Health

The population of Manchester city multiplied roughly ninefold during the first part of the nineteenth century from 10,000 to more than 88,000. The coming of the Industrial Revolution with its insatiable demand for labour led to a programme of rapid house-building on a large scale. During the first four decades of the century, before building regulations were introduced in the 1840s, the aim was to build as many houses as possible, as cheaply as possible and as quickly as possible.

Space, ventilation and sanitation facilities were very much secondary considerations, hence the rows of small back-to-backs, the infamous 'courts' and the proximity to the 'dark Satanic Mills'. There were few 'water closets', or flushing toilets as they are better known today. There were large numbers of 'pail closets' where the contents of the pail would have to be emptied when full into either night waste collection carts or into the open sewers that frequently flooded. Sometimes one such toilet had to serve 300 people. Indoor flush toilets were usually the domain of the upper or middle classes. More affluent workers, whose houses were a little larger than the millworkers' shacks, often had outdoor toilets in a shed a few yards from the house. Although some notions of Victorian hygiene left much to be desired, they genuinely believed it was unhealthy to have indoor toilets. There was no clean piped water to many workers' individual houses either. Water had to be fetched from communal standpipes in the street. Attached to most of these pipes was a tin mug for folk to use for a drink. It was inevitable that infectious diseases such as fevers, smallpox, measles and whooping cough, TB, typhus and typhoid would spread rapidly in such an environment. Although Manchester's first hospital, the Infirmary, had been established in 1752 by a surgeon named Charles White and had proved to be a successful and competent institution, the general health of working-class Mancunians was appalling. Engels wrote that in the Irish community off Oxford Road there were 'women made unfit for childbearing, children deformed, men enfeebled, limbs crushed, whole generations wrecked, afflicted with disease and infirmity, purely to fill the pockets of bourgeoisie' (Friedrich Engels, 1842–44).

The first Medical Officer of Health was not appointed in Manchester until 1868, although this was not done out of philanthropic concern for the working classes, but when realization dawned that infectious diseases did not recognize class barriers and that the children of the upper classes were also at risk. One in five Manchester men was condemned as unfit when enlistment for the Boer War (1899–1902) took place. Menstruation, pregnancy and childbirth were simply a nightmare for many women; the infant mortality rate before the Great War rose to almost half of all live births. Even in the twenty-first century, life expectancy for both sexes is lower in Manchester than in many other parts of the country. However, Manchester's health issues were revolutionized by James Niven who became Medical Officer of Health for the city in 1922. He insisted on several improvements in housing standards, disposal of sewage and refuse, milk and water supply, as well as tackling smoke pollution. As a result, he reduced the death rate in Manchester from 24.26 to 13.82 per 1,000 of the population.

Childbirth was dangerous and becoming a mother (first-time or otherwise) was a problem for many Manchester women in the Industrial Revolution. In the nineteenth century the correlation between hygiene and infant or maternal mortality had not been fully realized by most, even members of the medical profession. St Mary's Hospital for Women and Children was established in 1790 by Dr White on Old Bridge Street in Salford, just across the city border, before moving to Quay Street, then to Oxford Street and on to Oxford Road. It was originally known as the Manchester Lying-in Hospital and Charity for the Delivery of Poor Women at their own Habitations. Wealthier women had home births as a matter of course but there was little provision for such an event in the cramped, often damp surroundings of the small workers' cottages. The 'lying-in period' was conventionally a fortnight; sometimes a month. During this time the mother would stay in bed, recovering from the birth and tending to her baby. However, many working-class women simply could not afford to take so much time off work because there was no paid maternity leave and paternity leave was a foreign concept that belonged to the future. They had little option but to return to work within a day or two. Wet nurses could usually be found for the baby due to the high infant mortality rate and grieving mothers who were not working would oblige by feeding someone else's baby themselves. Wet nurses were also in demand from upper-class mothers who did not feel it quite the done thing to feed their baby themselves. For working-class mothers and the very poor in the city there was also the difficult question of nappies. Until the late 1970s there were no disposable nappies and it was only from the late 1950s onwards that washing machines became common. By the mid-twentieth century babies usually wore two nappies pinned together around them with safety pins: the outer one made of terry towelling for absorption; the inner one made of muslin which was soft and smooth against the baby's skin. Dirty nappies had to be soaked in disinfectant and then put on a boil-wash, done in the copper (a large heated tub in the scullery for those that had one) or a large stove-top pan. During the nineteenth and early twentieth centuries middle and upper-class women often had servants to do this unpleasant task for them, but in the tiny cramped cottages of the millscapes with their limited facilities it was a problem. Old rags or threadbare towelling or even pieces of sacking were used as nappies, cut into large squares and tied around the baby's middle. Dirty nappies were rinsed out by mothers as best they could, but sometimes nappies that were just wet were simply dried and put back on the baby. In the early and mid-nineteenth century there was little correlation between the ideas of hygiene and infant mortality.

However, towards the end of the nineteenth century and into the first decades of the twentieth century, mother-and-baby classes were organized by the City Council and run by women, most of them mothers themselves. Many first-time mothers had little idea of how to care for their babies properly and the classes did much to reduce the number of children dying in their first year of life. While it was considered quite fit and proper for women to advise other women on baby and child care and for female midwives to supervise births, there was resistance to the idea of female doctors. It was best left to men to decide upon the arrangements attending birth. Henry Fry, in his book *Maternity* published in 1907, advocates 'sterilisation of the appropriate areas', which is admirable, but he then goes on to explain why pain mitigation was inadvisable:

> The relief of pain during childbirth removes the maternal instinct... and it is immoral because it produces a condition similar to intoxication...various ill effects are attributed to it...epilepsy, convulsions and insanity...it is sacrilegious to thrust aside the decrees of providence...woman has been sentenced to suffer the pangs of childbirth, and it would rob God of the deep, earnest cries which arise in time of trouble for help.

Dr John Gunn in his 1861 book *Gunn's New Domestic Physician* also has some rather alarming ideas. He writes: 'the parts of generation during labour should always be well oiled or greased with lard, as it greatly assists and mitigates the suffering, and lubricates the parts of passage.' Henry Fry's views sum up the Victorian idea that women had to be punished in some way for simply being women. Victorian male views on female feelings, love, sexual activity and procreation were repressive, designed to subjugate women entirely, and were, most of all, immensely hypocritical. The overriding theme was that men were never, ever, in any way responsible for any sexual matters. 'Boys will be boys' was the general platitude but 'girls had to be perfect.' Some Victorian men took it to extremes, insisting that women should not be allowed to ride horses or bicycles as such activities 'might encourage certain female desires.' It was fine for boys to gain pre-marital sexual experience by sleeping around but any woman who was not 'chaste, pure and a virgin on her wedding night' was a 'fallen woman' who should be socially shunned. Quite how they believed their boys should gain their experience and with whom was never discussed. Illegitimacy was a major stigma for both mother and child and it continued to be so up until the 1970s. If a girl became pregnant, all the boy had to do was deny paternity and he was usually believed. It was always the girl who had to bear the brunt of birthing and the cost of bringing up the child on her own. Often her disgusted parents would throw her out of the house so that she had no home either. It was her 'punishment' for allowing her feelings to take their natural course. Their main option was a mother-and-baby home where they would stay until the child was born. These homes were often run by nuns and were usually spartan. The girls had to work hard for their living, frequently in the laundries run by the convents. After the birth many of the babies were adopted, with or without the mother's consent. It was a brutal system but it seemed no one was prepared 'to rob God of the deep earnest cries which arise in time of trouble for help', as Henry Fry put it.

However, someone did note 'the deep earnest cries for help' from mothers and children. Dr Catherine Chisholm was born in Radcliffe, Lancashire, not far from Manchester, but she spent most of her life in Manchester. She gained a BA in Classics from Owens College (the Victoria University of Manchester) and a year later, in 1889, she became the first female student at the Owens College Medical School. She was also the first female medical student to graduate from Manchester University, having gained a first-class degree in forensic medicine, obstetrics, surgery and pathology. Her father was a GP and very supportive of her ambition to practise medicine. Catherine Chisholm's first residency was as medical officer at Clapham Maternity Hospital which, most unusually for the time, employed only female doctors. Returning to Manchester in 1906, she became a GP for female students at the university and, subsequently, a physician for children at Manchester's Northern Hospital, as well as a consultant at both Hope Hospital in Salford and at the Manchester Babies Hospital which she established and staffed entirely with female doctors. Dr Chisholm committed her whole life to women's and children's medical issues, and she lectured for more than twenty-five years at Manchester University on childhood diseases and the importance of vaccination. Flying in the face of Victorian principles, she advocated sporting activities for women and founded the Women Students' and Athletics Union at Manchester University. She was the school medical officer for Manchester Girls' High School from 1908 to 1945 and the medical officer for female students at Manchester University from 1918 to 1947. Catherine Chisholm also wrote a book, *The Medical Inspection of Girls in Secondary Schools*, in which she discussed and promoted understanding of menstruation for young women at a time when the subject was still very much taboo. She was appointed medical adviser on child health to the Public Health Committee where she worked with Margaret Ashton, the city's first female councillor, who in turn assisted with funding for the Babies' Hospital. Dr Chisholm's legacy, as well as her work for women's issues and children's medical care, was the establishment in 1947 of the Chair in Child Health at Manchester University, and after her death in 1952 the *British Medical Journal* made a successful subscription appeal which endowed the Catherine Chisholm Memorial Lecture.

Dr Eleanor Schill, born in 1904 at Withington Hall in Manchester, was an early medical student at Manchester University as well as Dr Chisholm. After university she became a committee member for the McAlpine home for unmarried mothers in Manchester and also the Princess Christian College which offered courses in childcare qualifications. In 1939 she attended the initial meeting of the Marriage Guidance Council and, having taken a diploma in psychiatry, she became a counsellor in the late 1940s for those whose marriages were in trouble, her specialisms being 'education before and within marriage'. Shortly after the Second World War Dr Schill also became the school doctor for Manchester High School for Girls and, with their shared interests in women's and children's issues, she would have undoubtedly known Catherine Chisholm and perhaps worked with her.

Another major health problem for women was the question of sexually transmitted diseases (STDs). These were always seen as solely the fault of the female sex. Women suffering from STDs could be imprisoned and sentenced to hard labour. Men were not held accountable in any way. There was an epidemic of STDs during the Great War, the responsibility for which General Sir Douglas Haig laid completely at women's door, claiming that his troops were 'exceedingly chaste, innocent and pure' and had been 'utterly defiled by wicked women'. The police in the late 1800s were harsh with women they suspected of having STDs. They were taken to the local police station where a male police officer would subject them to a rough, often painful, manual examination of their intimate areas before forcibly inserting a cold steel speculum to examine them internally. The reformer Josephine Butler dubbed it 'steel rape' and fought hard for amendments to the Contagious Diseases Acts. Women who were subjected to these examinations might actually be clean, healthy and totally innocent of what they were accused, but the fact of having undergone such an examination ruined their reputations so that no one would employ them and this actually forced some of them into prostitution to earn a living. Butler found a lot of support among working-class men, because working-class women were particularly harassed in this manner in Manchester, especially those from the poverty-stricken Ancoats, Angel Meadow and Little Ireland localities. However, some of the pimps who lived off the immoral earnings of the prostitutes under their control pelted her with cow dung in protest. The bias of the legislation against women was generally explained by stating that 'there is no comparison to be made between prostitutes and the men who consort with them…with the one sex the offence is committed as a matter of gain; with the other it is an irregular indulgence of a natural impulse.'

Josephine Butler was not a Mancunian (she was born in Northumberland and married to an Oxford don) but she spent some time in Liverpool with her husband who had been appointed headmaster of Liverpool College. She was a firm supporter of female suffrage, believing that women would benefit immensely from better education and, together with another suffragist supporter, Anne Clough, she helped to establish the North of England Council for Promoting the Higher Education of Women. She also campaigned hard for legal recognition of married women until the Married Women's Property Act was passed in 1882, and she continued to campaign for the amendments to the Contagious Diseases Act, backed by the Norfolk feminist writer Harriet Martineau and by Florence Nightingale, until finally, in 1885, the 'compulsory examination of women' under the Contagious Diseases Acts was repealed.

The slur on women remained, however. Any woman that a man considered to be poorly-dressed or talking inappropriately could be deemed a whore. Any woman living with a man to whom she was not married was considered a prostitute. In fact, any female who did not conform to the strict conventional attitudes was considered 'loose, unsuitable, unpleasant, and probably a whore.' Victorian attitudes were slow to subside. As late as the 1980s there were still those who frowned upon the practice of girls working away from home in the towns and cities, flat-sharing or house-sharing. Among many of the older generation it was considered that 'nice girls stayed at home with mother until they married.' Some girls who did leave mother to